F IN

EXAMS

THE BIG BOOK OF TEST PAPER BLUNDERS

Richard Benson

summersdale

F IN EXAMS

The contents of this book were first published between 2008 and 2015 by Summersdale Publishers Ltd, under the titles *F in Exams*, *F in English*, *F in Geography*, *F in History*, *F in Science*, *F in Retakes*, *F in School*, *F in Spelling* and *F in Exams Joke Book*.

This edition copyright © Summersdale Publishers Ltd, 2016

Summersdale Publishers Ltd
46 West Street
Chichester
West Sussex
PO19 1RP
UK

www.summersdale.com

Printed and bound in the Czech Republic

ISBN: 978-1-84953-924-1

Contents

Introduction

The attitude of today is 'trying is as good as succeeding' and these perplexed pupils certainly do give it a good old go. English, music, maths, science, history... there's no end to the subjects that today's bright young things are baffled by. Still, even if these exam howlers score a zero on the exam, they score a big laugh from us. After all, who hasn't taken a swing and missed on a test before? Some of these answers may make you cringe, but it will be in sympathy, as you remember the time your teacher had to tell you 'I'm afraid that reindeers are not mythical creatures'.

This collection brings together the best of the *F in Exams* series plus all-new content guaranteed to make you howl – mostly with laughter!

Subject: **Science**

Subject: Chemistry

What is a nitrate?

It is much cheaper than a day rate.

Give a brief explanation of the meaning of the term 'hard water'.

Ice

What is a vacuum?

Something my Mum says I should use more often.

What is the process where steam turns into water?

Conversation

What is methane?

Methane is a smelly greenhouse gas which is produced when trees and/or cows are burned.

In a blast furnace it is impossible for aluminium to be extracted from its ores. Why?

Because it is bloomin' hot!

Over the last 50 years there has been a significant change in the concentration of carbon dioxide. Give a reason for this.

It's easily distracted.

What are the characteristics of crude oil?

 Coarse and crude

Describe the chemical differences between H_2O and CO_2.

H_2O is hot water,
CO_2 is cold water

Describe a neutrino.

The opposite of an oldtrino.

Define an alloy.

The fancy bit on a car wheel.

What is a polymer?

A group of mermaids.

What is the purpose of chromatography?

To take pictures of time.

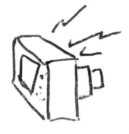 

What nutrient is known for helping to produce healthy bones and teeth?

Bread crusts
(that's what my granny says)

What would be the best way to neutralise the effects of acid rain?

Alkaseltzer.

Explain the term 'half-life'.

When someone only goes out and has fun half the time.

Describe a radioisotope.

A device for listening to the stars

Science

Why is sodium stored under oil?

So it doesn't have as far to fall if you knock the packet over.

What happens to iron oxide in a blast furnace?

It gets hot

What does a covalent bond involve?

a secret friendship between nuns

In comparison with large hydrocarbons, how would you describe small hydrocarbons?

They are smaller.

What process is used to purify copper?

Exorcism.

Why are potassium and sodium in the same group in the periodic table?

Because they are BFFs.

Where are vegetable oils found?

In the oils aisle.

What is mayonnaise an example of?

Salad dressing

Give an example of an emulsion.

Dulux

What is the symbol for iron?

What is the purpose of a fractioning column?

A column with fractions is useless, because it wouldn't hold anything up.

What is an artificial pesticide?

Someone who is only pretending to be annoying really.

Name a metal element that burns with a bright white light.

Magneto.

What is the carbon cycle?

An expensive kind of bike.

Give two examples of hydrocarbons.

Pepsi & Coke

What do we call the chemical reaction between a fuel and an oxidant when heated?

FIRE! I love fire.

What is the process in which sugars convert to gases, acids and/or alcohol?

Puberty

What are nanoparticles?

> The tiny pieces that grannies are made of

Explain why diamonds are hard. What can diamonds be used for?

> They're hard to stop your jewellery getting damaged. They can be used for rings, watches and tooth implants.

Why is methane a gas at 20° Celsius?

> Because that's the temperature of a fart.

Who was Humphry Davy? What did he invent?

He fell off a wall before he could invent anything.

Why is Mars red?

Because it's embarrassed about Uranus.

Why does bread need to prove?

It has an insecurity complex. It should really be happy as it is.

Subject: .... **Biology**

What is the highest frequency noise that a human can register?

Mariah Carey.

Adam cuts his arm. Blood gushes out and is red in colour. What does this show?

He is not a robot, he's a real boy!

What is a fibula?

A little lie

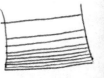

What is the meaning of the word 'varicose'?

Close by

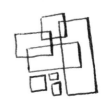

What does 'terminal illness' mean?

when you become ill at the airport.

What happens when your body starts to age?

when you get old your organs work less effectively and you can go intercontinental.

What happens during puberty to a boy?

He says goodbye to his childhood and enters adultery.

What are the three different types of blood vessels?

Vanes, anchovies and caterpillars.

Karen goes into her garden one morning and finds the leaves covered in a sticky substance. What is this substance?

When the leaves sit in the sunshine they get hot and it makes them sweat.

What is a plasmid?

A high definition television

How is oxygen loaded, transported and unloaded in the bloodstream?

Big forklift truck

Explain the concept of homeostasis.

It is when you stay at home all day and don't go out.

Draw a diagram to represent the human body and label the positions of all the major organs including: brain, heart, lungs and kidneys.

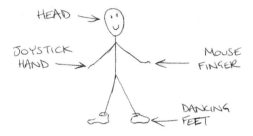

Draw a diagram indicating the location of the appendix.

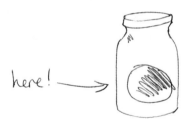

Below is a diagram of the heart. Please label the relevant sections.

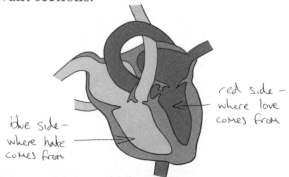

What is a fossil?

A fossil is the remains of an extinct animal. The older the fossil, the more extinct the animal is.

What happens to your body when taking a breath?

Your chest gets bigger.

What is the world's largest living mammal?

The woolly mammoth

Different living organisms reproduce in different ways. Describe two methods of reproduction.

The Stork and Angel Gabriel

What is meant by microorganism?

A very small keyboard

How does the process of natural selection work?

The two captains just have to go with their instincts to pick their teams.

What are the properties of crude oil?

It's rude and has no manners.

What are the negative effects of global dimming?

Everybody gets thicker

What are the effects of rearing cattle?

Getting kicked in the teeth.

Explain the process of evolution.

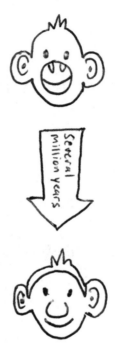

What is likely to happen to an individual that is poorly suited to its environment?

He's bought a new suit

Why are white peppered moths likely to be more common than black ones in country areas?

Racism.

What causes tectonic plates to move?

Noisy neighbours.

Which is the most abundant gas in the atmosphere?

farts.

What is meant by the term 'biodiversity'?

IT'S A DOUBLE UNIVERSITY

Describe the properties of a meteor.

An animal that only eats meat.

The island of Madagascar houses many species that are not found anywhere else on the planet. Give one possible explanation for this.

Why would they Move? Madagascar is ace!

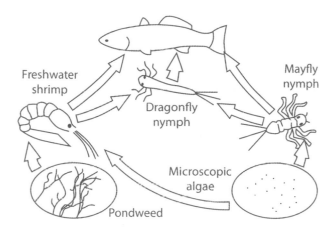

In this food web, what is represented by the arrows?

Who fancies who.

There has been a marked rise in the percentage of carbon dioxide in the Earth's atmosphere over the last 50 years; suggest one reason for this.

Breathing.

What is chlorophyll?

An ingredient in expensive shampoo.

Explain the process of eutrophication.

It's when a country joins the Euro.

Describe the purpose of cytoplasm.

In Ghostbusters II it was used to make the Statue of Liberty come to life. I've never seen it used since.

Describe the purpose of antibodies.

They are married to Uncle bodies

What changes take place in a girl during puberty?

SHE GETS BOOBS AND GETS STROPPY.

What is the meaning of the terms 'density dependent' and 'density independent'?

Density dependent is when you are thick and live at home. Density independent is when you are a bit less thick and live on your own.

Where in the human body is the humerus found?

It changes because everyone's humerus is different.

Give an example of a disease caused by fungi.

Mushroomitis.

What is meant by the term 'placebo effect'?

TECHNICAL TERM FOR WHAT HAPPENS WHEN PEOPLE GO 'EMO'.

Describe the function of red blood cells.

To keep blood the
right colour.

What is meant by immunity?

You can do bad things
and get away with it.

What can vaccination involve?

Going to the beach,
Swimming, good food.

It is important to use antibiotics carefully because...

You'll run out of biotics.

What are the key differences between aerobic and anaerobic respiration?

'an'

Give two similarities between an eye and a camera.

1. The round bit
2. They both blink.

Give one reason why MRSA is causing problems in hospitals.

Mr. Sa is always causing problems because he is rude and noisy.

What is a fistula?

A mini fist

Before taking blood, a nurse dabs some alcohol onto the patient's arm. This makes the patient's skin feel cold. Explain what happens to make the patient's skin feel cold.

A nurse dabs some alcohol onto the patient's arm.

Coronary heart disease is an illness affected by hereditary factors. Name two hereditary factors that affect our health.

Your mum's health and your dad's health.

Your body needs to keep an internal temperature of 37°C. Name one way your body cools itself down if your temperature goes above 37°C.

TURNS THE HEATING DOWN

Science

How are inherited factors passed from generation to generation?

By writing a will.

What is the purpose of bile?

When you want to show someone you're angry.

COOL!

What part of the body is affected by glandular fever?

The glandular.

43

When an organism's genetic material spontaneously changes, what is it called? Give an example.

An X-man. When Logan grew bone claws and changed his name to Wolverine.

Name two types of fat found in food.

1. GOOD FAT
2. BAD FAT

Name the five senses.

1 Nonsense
2 Suspense
3 Insense
4 CommonSense
5 Seeing Ghosts

What is the generic term for birds that hunt for food primarily via flight?

Birds that pray.

Explain the meaning of the word 'myopic'.

It's when someone makes a biopic, but about themselves.

Give an example of a meal that might contain a high level of protein.

Grilled chicken beast with vegetables

What's the scientific term for a living thing?

An Orgasm

Name some of the purposes of antibiotics.

To protect against biotics.

What body part expands and contracts in order to allow the human body to control the movements of its limbs?

Mussels

Explain how plants compete.

Most plants play fair,
but Venus flytraps bite.

Explain why Darwin's theories were unpopular when
they were first published.

He suggested humans
are descended from
apps.

What is a pathogen?

A killer gene

Why is it important to help prevent the extinction of plant species?

BECAUSE OTHERWISE WE'LL NEVER EVOLVE TRIFFIDS IN REAL LIFE.

What are the negative effects of regularly smoking cannabis?

It makes your clothes smell

You run out of money

Regularly running out of cannabis

Steve is driving his car. He is travelling at 60 feet/second and the speed limit is 40 mph. Is Steve speeding?

He could find out by checking his speedometer.

Explain the word 'momentum'.

A brief moment

What was Sir Isaac Newton famous for?

He invented gravity.

When a star's life cycle is over there is a possibility it will become a black hole. Describe a 'black hole'.

Something very dark in the ground and it looks like this ⊃

Many people don't like eating radiation-treated food. How could a food scientist prove that radiation-treated food is safe?

By eating some!

Name an environmental side effect of burning fossil fuels.

Fire

Describe what happened during the 'big bang'.

A lot of noise.

Give the names of two gases that might contribute to global warming.

1. Bottom gas

2. Cow burps

Hannah sprays her new bike purple. The spraying of the bike gives it a negative charge and the paint a positive one. Why is this?

Positive – spraying is easier than using a paintbrush.

Negative – purple isn't a good colour for a bike.

What does the National Grid do?

Cooks sausages to perfection.

What does a transformer do?

It can go from being a robot to a dragster in three seconds.

Give an example of a step-up transformer.

An exercise machine

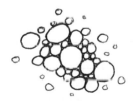

 IN EXAMS

Give a reason why people would want to live near power lines.

You get your electricity faster.

Give three ways to reduce heat loss in your home.

1. Thermal underwear
2. Move to Hawaii
3. Close the door

What instrument do you use to measure temperature?

A trombone.

54

Why are catalytic converters fitted to cars?

To make sure no cats get run over.

What is beta radiation?

Radiation that's nearly complete, but needs to be tested.

Explain how a vehicle can be designed to reduce friction.

It could secrete grease.

Draw the electronic component symbol for a switch.

Explain the difference between a discrete variable and a categoric variable.

Discrete variables are quite secretive where as categoric variables are rather blunt.

When conducting a study, what is the purpose of a control group?

To tell the others what to do.

Explain the process of thermal energy transfer.

Cuddles

What is the distance from the crest of one wave to the crest of the next wave called?

The sea.

Describe the properties of a thermosoftening plastic.

It gets soft when you put it in a flask with hot tea.

At the end of a marathon, a runner covers herself in a silvered space blanket. Explain how the space blanket helps keep the runner warm.

Alien technology.

Give one advantage, in any research project, of having a large sample size rather than a small sample size.

You can see it better.

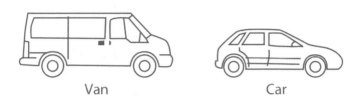

Van   Car

The diagram shows a van and a car. The two vehicles have the same mass and identical engines. Explain why the top speed of the car is greater than the top speed of the van.

It has go-faster stripes.

When taking an X-ray, why does the radiographer go behind a screen?

Privacy.

Name one key use of a plane mirror.

CHECK YOUR HAIR LOOKS GOOD AT
THE END OF THE JOURNEY.

Explain the process of bioleaching.

It's when you
choose natural bleach.

A student hears the sound waves produced by an ambulance siren. When the ambulance is stationary, the student hears a constant frequency. When the ambulance moves away from the student, the sound they hear changes. What is the name of this effect?

The doppleganger effect.

An astronomer uses a telescope to observe the movement of stars and planets. Give one advantage of having a telescope at the top of a high mountain rather than the bottom.

The mountain doesn't get in the way.

What is the key use for thermochromic plastic, and why?

To make cool stuff that changes colour.

?

What is an electric current?

A zingy fruit.

Where and how are fossil fuels extracted?

Mostly by grinding up old dinosaurs.

What are lasers used for?

The main weapon on the Millennium Falcon

How is burning fossil fuels harmful to the atmosphere?

The smoke makes you cough.

What type of electricity production harnesses the power of the sea?

Turtle power

Explain ways that a household energy bill can be reduced.

Tear it into small pieces

What determines the pitch of a sound?

How angry the person making it is.

Why do the windows steam up on the inside of a car on a wet day?

> Because it's too rainy to snog outside, so people have to do it in their cars.

How does a puddle of water disappear after a rain shower?

> It ejaculates.

What does 'thinking distance' mean in terms of a vehicle stopping?

> It's the distance you drive when you think of something you left at home and you have to stop and go back for it.

What affects braking distance?

It depends on when you last stopped for a brake.

How does an earth wire protect the user of an electrical appliance?

It's packed full of earth so no electricity can pass through it.

Why are earth wires used in electrical appliances?

Because we're trying to be eco-friendly and use nature's resources.

Give one reason why copper is used on the base of saucepans.

It looks nice when they're hanging up.

What force draws objects away from the centre of rotation?

The Force (dark side).

Explain the term 'quantum entanglement'.

A complicated mess.

Why can dogs hear sounds that we can't?

We don't know what sounds they hear because we can't hear them?

It's said that all the matter that makes up the human race could fit in a sugar cube. Why is this?

Everyone loves sugar – it's all that matters.

What is the hardest natural material known to man?

Rocks.

Subject: **Geography**

RM
4
TS

Subject: .... **Human Geography** ....

Geography

Explain the dispersal of various farming types in Britain.

The cows + pigs are distributed in different fields so they don't eat each other

Explain what is meant by the term 'pastoral farming'.

It's a farm run by vicars.

Define the phrase 'commercial farming'.

It is when a farmer advertises his farm on T.V to get more customers.

Define the term 'intensive farming'.

It is when a farmer never has a day off.

Explain the word 'migration'.

Migration is a bad headache.

What do we call a person forced to leave their home, perhaps by a natural disaster or war, without having another home to go to?

Homeless

Define the term 'shanty town'.

It is a place where people like beer with lemonade in it.

Define the phrase 'heavy industry'.

An industry that sells tons.

What was the main industry in Persia?

Cats

The race of people known as Malays come from which country?

Malaria

Inhabitants of Moscow are called...

Mosquitoes

Name one of the primary products of the Hawaiian Islands.

Grass skirts and flower necklaces

Geography

What is the collective name given to the inhabitants of the Philippine islands?

The Philistines

Name one technique used by farmers to improve crop yield.

Farmers mostly increase crops by irritating the land.

What are the Pyramids?

The Pyramids are a large mountain range which splits France and Spain

Turkey has seen a fall in its levels of export trade. Give one possible reason for this.

A rise in vegetarianism — turkeys being eaten less.

Everest base camp is an example of an extreme environment visited by tourists. Give two reasons why tourists visit extreme environments.

1. They didn't read the brochure
2. They want to impress their friends

Give two reasons people would visit Iceland.

1. Cheap food
2. Good advertising.

What are wooden barriers built at right-angles to the beach called?

fences.

Name a way of protecting a coastal area from flooding.

Armed police

Some people agree with the building of coastal defences while others disagree with it. Why is this?

Some people will disagree with anything.

What is the purpose of dams?

Similar to blast and gah.

What public services does a youthful population put a strain on?

Beer
Traffic cones
Shopping trollies

Explain the increase in demand for water and electricity in the south of England.

They're thirsty and keep getting bigger TVs.

Why does population naturally change over time?

It gets bored.

Describe two ways of reducing the demand for water.

1. When it's yellow let it mellow
2. When it's brown flush it down.

What tends to happen to a country's carbon footprint as it develops?

IT GETS DARKER.

What does feedback in an industrial system involve?

A loud, high-pitched noise.

What is secondary industry?

Not as good as primary industry.

Which sector employs the most people in the UK?

The job sector.

Name a factor which might attract a multinational corporation to a country.

Nice beaches.

Name two economic indicators.

Left blinker and right blinker.

What does the term population distribution refer to?

The spread of fizzy drinks throughout the country.

What is meant by population density?

How stupid people are.

How many people could there be on the planet by 2025?

None – the world will end in 2017

Describe one major problem caused by counter-urbanisation.

The urbanisers might get angry.

Geography

Describe some ways that pollution problems could be reduced in cities in poorer parts of the world.

Get rid of the cows.

What does CBD stand for?

Currently Bored Dizzy

Explain why the number of food miles is increasing.

PEOPLE DEMAND FREE-RANGE, SO THE CHICKENS RUN MORE MILES EVERY DAY.

What is GNP?

A far right political party

What is a nucleated village?

One that's close to a nuclear power station.

What factors affect the sustainability of food sources?

How much people like the taste of them.

Describe the process of irrigation.

When a farmer irritates his crops they grow faster

Give a reason for the decline in employment in primary and secondary industries in the UK.

Less children.

Name one advantage of quarrying.

Any disagreements are out in the open and can be dealt with.

Name one disadvantage of quarrying.

Sometimes it ends in tears, or blows.

Name one way in which the impact of quarrying can be reduced.

Softer hammers.

What is a brownfield site?

A site with no grass, just mud.

Geography

Explain the terms 'subsistence farming' and 'nomadic farming'.

One is underground and the other is done by gnomes.

Give one positive aspect of organic farming.

The organic labels look prettier

What is meant by 'pull' and 'push' factors?

How strong the teams are in a tug of war.

What is 'agri-business'?

A bad way of running your business as you might lose customers.

What is the difference between 'hard' and 'soft' engineering techniques?

The consistency.

Describe the characteristics of shanty houses.

1. Near the seaside
2. Full of people who like singing

Geography

The development of greenfield sites can threaten the countryside. Explain why this can be the case.

Greenfield sites are
very aggressive.

Explain two possible causes of rural depopulation.

1. No-one fancies farmers
2. People leave because the countryside smells funny.

What is meant by 'the development gap'?

The time it takes for you to get your photos back from the shop.

What is 'stewardship'?

Difficult times for beef stews, lamb stews etc.

What is meant by the term ecotourism?

Travelling to Bognor Regis by coach.

Geography

What is the name of Germany's fourth-largest city?

Colon .

What sort of clothing would you associate with Scottish national dress?

Scottish people like to wear twee jackets and quilts.

Subject: **Physical Geography**

What scale do seismologists use to measure the force of earthquakes?

A very strong one
(not glass).

Volcanoes occur on what kind of plate margins?

Hot plates.

What happens at the edge of a destructive plate margin?

It breaks!

Name the area of calm at the centre of a storm?

The pie in the sky.

What does the word 'lava' mean?

A pre-pubescent caterpillar

Explain the meaning of the word 'magma'.

Japanese cartoons.

THIS WAY

Geography

What is meant by 'a pull factor'?

A big red sports car.

Name the smaller rivers which run into the Nile.

The Juveniles.

Which artificial waterway runs between the Mediterranean and Red seas?

The Savage Canal.

Name one measure which can be put into place to avoid river flooding in times of extensive rainfall (e.g. in Mississippi).

Flooding in areas such as the mississippi may be avoided by placing a number of big dames into the river

How high is Mount Everest?

Depends how much snowfall it has had since it was last measured.

The Narmada and the Tapi river valleys are said to be old rift valleys. What is a rift valley?

Valleys that have fallen out after an argument.

Geography

Where can you find the Andes?

Google Earth.

What methods are used for preserving rainforest?

Pickling

What is afforestation?

When the train stops in the forests.

~~~~

Describe two negative effects of a drought.

1. No swimming
2. No wet T-shirt competitions.

Where are temperate deciduous forests found?

In places that are not too hot or cold.

What are plants that are able to store water called?

Clever.

Geography

Where are deserts found?

In the chilled aisle

What is salinisation?

Cleaning.

Name one cause of avalanches.

Yodelling

How are sedimentary rocks formed?

That's sedimentary, my dear Watson.

Photos of the Alps show that glaciers have retreated over the last 50 years. One reason for this could be climate change. What could another reason be?

They're shy.

Describe the greenhouse effect.

When you get old and spend all your time in the greenhouse, tending plants.

Geography

Why is it helpful to leave dead wood to rot?

Because if you use it to build things it breaks.

What does a choropleth map show?

location of choropleths.

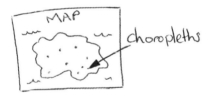

What does it mean if a waterfall has an overhang?

Not enough exercise, too many chips

What is the hydrological cycle also known as?

Clever water bike.

How much of the world's water is stored in seas and oceans?

A LOT.

What is a confluence?

When two things happen at the same time, unexpectedly.

Geography

What is the mouth of a river?

It is how the river eats.

What is the watershed?

Where fish do DIY.

What is created when a river runs over alternating layers of hard and soft rock?

Glam rock.

Name one key force of change in a coastal system.

THE R.N.L.I.

How are waves created?

1. Lift your arm.
2. Shake your hand back and forth.

What is the distance a wave has travelled called?

The sea.

Geography

When is deposition likely to occur?

When you are
at the bank

What is a storm surge?

When the gods get angry.

Boom!

What is the direction of longshore drift?

UP.

There are many different ways in which the sea erodes the coast. Explain two ways in which the sea erodes the coast.

1. Nibbling
2. Biting

What is a groyne?

A noise of pain.

What environmental factors can cause plate slippage?

Loose table legs.

Geography

What is slumping?

Bad posture.

What do the geological time periods relate to?

We have geography at 11am on Wednesdays and Fridays.

Which part of the Earth is directly below the crust?

The filling

Describe the different phases of the rock cycle.

It developed from Rythym and Blues and Jazz, into Rock'n'Roll and then into Rock.

Name a characteristic of metamorphic rock.

Changeable.

Name a characteristic of igneous rock.

Very clever.

Which part of the Earth is the hottest?

Africa.

Give two differences between continental crust and oceanic crust.

One is on French pizza, the other is on seafood pizza.

How are fold mountains formed?

Origami.

What is the name for professionals who monitor and predict volcanic eruptions?

Vulcans

Give an example of a supervolcano.

What is a tsunami?

a move in sumo wrestling

What is the name for the scientific practice of studying the atmosphere and monitoring and predicting the weather and climate?

Being a weather man.

Where do hurricanes normally form?

In the air.

What is meant by extreme weather?

When you have to stay indoors

December 2010 is one example of extreme weather in the UK. What was December 2010 a period of?

Winter

Draw an annotated diagram to explain the process of relief rainfall.

What does the term latitude refer to?

It's french for attitude

How are deserts formed?

My favourite way is to combine ice cream, sliced bananas, caramel sauce and lots of squirty cream.

What are the Nazca Lines?

Nazca is a really popular sport in America. Lines are drawn on the road to show drivers where to go.

How do you know when a tsunami is about to occur?

The weather presenter tells you.

What causes can there be for environmental change?

When coins drop out of people's pockets while they're walking in the countryside.

What are the characteristics of a shield volcano?

It's the one that protects all the other volcanoes

How may a quarry be used for tourism purposes?

It's a great day out for tourists who like rocks.

Describe the effects of perceived climate change.

The main one is that people perceive that the climate is changing.

Explain how heavy snow can cause disruption to daily life.

People get distracted from their work by snowball fights

$$\frac{\sqrt{5}}{5} = \sqrt{}$$

2 + 2 = 5

Subject: ....**Maths**.........................

Change 7/8 to a decimal.

7.8

Name a regular triangle.

a three - sided triangle.

Maths

Find the angles marked with letters.

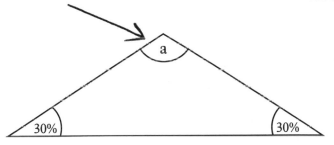

THIS IS THE ANGLE MARKED WITH A LETTER

a

30% 30%

Write two hundred thousand in figures.

two hundred thousand in figures.

119

What is a six-sided polygon known as?

an empty cage

There are 300 students in Year 10. Mary and Mark want to find out Year 10's favourite colour.
Mary asks 30 people.
Mark asks 150 people.
Mark says 'My conclusions are more likely to be reliable than Mary's'.
Why does Mark think he is right?

Because Mark is a man

A car company is having a sale. A car that was £25,000 before the sale now has 50 per cent off. What is the new price?

Still too expensive.

Expand 2(x + y).

$2(x+y)$

$2(x+y)$

$2(x+y)$

$2(x+y)$

Simplify the following equation.

$$\sqrt{\dfrac{5}{5}}$$

$$\dfrac{\sqrt{5}}{5} = \sqrt{}$$

x is inversely proportional to the square of y.
x=3 and y=4
Express x in terms of y.

$$:-x + :-y = :-)$$

Maths

What is conditional probability?

Maybe, maybe not

What is the splitting formula?

boy meets girl → boy meets another girl
→ Girl finds out about other Girl
= the splitting formula.
This is not to be confused with the spitting
formula, that's just antisocial.

What is a random variable?

Someone with multiple personalities

What is a discrete random variable?
Give an example with your answer.

It is a person that hides in the corner at parties. similar to the wall flower but a bit more unpredictable after a few drinks.

You are at a friend's party. Six cupcakes are distributed among nine plates, and there is no more than one cake per plate. What is the probability of receiving a plate with a cake on it?

Nil, if my sister is invited too.

What is the symbol for Pi?

← Pi!

 IN EXAMS

John and Julie are both strong badminton players. Is it more probable that Julie will beat John in four games out of seven or five games out of nine?

She will win every game.
She is a girl – girls are
better at these things.

How should Julie play to minimise any loss?

Dirty!

Maths

Calculate a formula for winning the lottery.

buy a ticket -> watch the lottery programme -> turn over to Ant and Dec while the boring bit is on -> turn back to find out that you have missed the important bit -> get cross -> ask your parents what the numbers were -> they are mysteriously absent from the house and return three weeks later after jetting off round the world after cashing in your winnings

A block of metal is 4 cm tall, 5 cm long and 10 cm deep. What is the volume of the block?

Very quiet, unless dropped. Then very loud.

A block is weighed and found to be 200 g. What pressure would this size and shape exert if rested on its largest face?

Enough to squash its nose.

Calculate the mean of this group of numbers:
2, 12, 5, 8, 4, 19, 8

Eight looks quite mean.

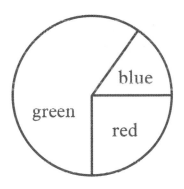

The diagram shows a fair spinner.
Which colour is the arrow least likely to land on?

Yellow

A hat costs £5 in the UK.

The same hat in Germany costs €8.00

The exchange rate is £1 = €1.40

Where would be cheaper to buy the hat from?

Taking the plane fare into account, the UK.

Give a two-digit square number smaller than 70.

Maths

If tickets to a football match cost £12.50 each, how much would it cost for Johnny and his three brothers to go.

£12.50 each

Lisa wants to knit two types of jumper, one requiring 2½ balls of wool and one requiring 1¾ balls, using only 4 balls of wool. Can she do it?

Only if she can actually knit.

Draw a polygon.

Oscar has three orange cards and nine green cards. What is the probability he picks a blue card?

9/12 if he's colour blind.

A town has a population of 80,000 to the nearest ten thousand.

What is the greatest possible population?

It depends on their combined achievements.

Samuel gets £15 a week for doing his chores. His parents increase this by £2 on his fourteenth birthday. What does he get after this?

A gambling problem.

A train that normally travels at an average of 60 mph leaves 30 minutes late. If it increases its average speed to 65 mph will it be on time?

No, trains are never on time.

Pasta	◯ ◯
Chilli	◯ ◿
Fish	◯ ◖
Curry	◖
Soup	

This pictogram shows the school lunches for the week.

Key: ◯ = 4 lunches

How many times was curry eaten in the week?

Pac - Man!

Ciara says that if she spins a spinner with an equal chance of landing on white, red, blue or green fifty times it will land on green four times. Is she correct? Explain your answer.

No.

Because Ciara is an idiot.

Draw a stem-and-leaf diagram to show the number of cups of tea consumed by a surveyed group of offices in a week:

46   12   4   83   25   9   60   42   34   36   19

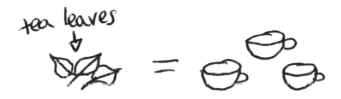

tea leaves

=

What are moving averages used for?

Maths on the go.

4 9 3 5

Use these digits to create:

a) The smallest four-digit number they can make:

4935

b) The largest four-digit number they can make:

4935

Maths

Write 7834 in words.

SEVEN EIGHT THREE FOUR

Draw a tetrahedron.

Draw a trapezium.

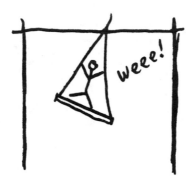

How do you calculate the volume of a prism?

Count all the prisoners.
The more prisoners,
the louder it will be.

Maths

What is the name of a six-sided polygon?

Sixagon

Two friends share £18 at a ratio of 6:3. How much do they each receive?

An unfair amount, if one friend is getting more than the other.

Is money 'continuous' or 'discrete'? Explain your answer.

My money is 'weekly' and 'pitiful'.

Write the number 32545346 in words.

Three two five four
five three four six

The probability that Steve oversleeps is three times the probability that he does not. Work out the probability that he does oversleep.

Depends - is it a Monday?

James' monthly outgoing costs are £50 on his mobile phone, £80 on utilities, £450 on rent and £80 on savings. Draw and label a pie chart to represent his outgoing costs.

Jane works in a cafe. She wants to work out if more men than women eat cake. Design an observation sheet for her.

Name three types of angle.

Charlie's Angles: Sabrina, Jill and Kelly.

Define a pentagram.

SOMETHING YOU USE TO SUMMON THE DEVIL.

Define a triangle.

The most boring instrument in the orchestra.

Subject: .... Reading Comprehension ....

Discuss the style of *Romeo and Juliet*.

It is written entirely in Islamic pentameter. The play is full of heroic couplets, one example being Romeo + Juliet themselves

How does Romeo's character develop throughout the play?

It doesn't, it's just self, self, self, all the way through.

In *Pride and Prejudice*, at what moment does Elizabeth Bennet realise her true feelings for Mr Darcy?

When she sees him coming out of the lake.

How does Dylan Thomas use voices to create an image of village life in Wales?

Putting on accents when he reads it out loud.

English

How are the mountain range's conditions described in *Touching the Void*?

> THE MOUNTAINS ARE PORTRAYED
> AS BEING HIGH AND POINTY,
> WITH SOME SNOWY PARTS
> AND SOME NOT SO

Do you think Heathcliff is an angry character? How has Brontë's writing influenced your opinion?

> Bronte invented Heathcliff, which is how she made us think he was angry.

What would you say was the key theme of *The Prime of Miss Jean Brodie*?

Maths and female mathematicians.

Give an example of sibilance in *Romeo and Juliet*.

Juliet and Tybalt are cousins but I don't think there are any sibilance.

List the main events of *Robinson Crusoe*.

Robinson goes on a cruise.

In what way is Pip an uncertain hero?

Because he's just not sure.

Provide an example of dramatic irony in *Othello*.

What is the overall message of *Frankenstein*?

Don't reanimate corpses.

What does *Heart of Darkness* say about the nature of humanity?

It's quite dark in nature for humans without any electricity.

What do you think makes Mercutio such a memorable character in *Romeo and Juliet*?

He lives inside a thermometer

Paraphrase the events of *Gulliver's Travels*.

Gulliver goes on holiday. He comes back, having enjoyed himself.

What is the significance of Dr Jekyll's door in *Dr Jekyll and Mr Hyde*?

It's the way he gets into Dr Jekyll's lab.

Why is isolation an important theme in Mary Shelley's *Frankenstein*?

When you're that ugly, isolation becomes a necessity.

Give an example of euphemism in *Midsummer Night's Dream*.

BOTTOM.

Name a key theme in *Madame Bovary*.

Cows

Summarise the events of *The Fall of the House of Usher*.

Building mishaps occur.

What are the main themes from *Sense and Sensibility*?

SENSES AND THE ABILITY
TO SENSE THINGS.

Explore a key theme from *Wuthering Heights*.

Cliffs

How is Piggy made sympathetic in *The Lord of the Flies*?

His little curly tail.

To what was Hemingway referring with the quote 'This isn't fun anymore'?

This exam.

What is the significance of the title of Orwell's Nineteen Eighty-Four?

That's when it was written.

List one or more characteristics of Gothic literature.

Black nail varnish.

Discuss the reasons for the main action of *Of Mice and Men* taking place over four days.

It is a short book, so doesn't take more than four days to read.

Give one famous quote from the play *Hamlet* which makes reference to Yorick?

The grand old duke of Yorick, he had ten thousand men...

How might the themes of *Crime and Punishment* be relevant to today's society?

It's been adapted into a TV show called Law and Order.

What is one of the key themes running through *The Diary of Anne Frank*?

> Anne Frank's Dairy had lots of cows running through it.

Lord of the Flies is often described as 'terrifying'. Describe an incident in the book which is terrifying.

> The bit where all the flies come out at once is quite scary, but it's hardly The Evil Dead.

What are your first impressions of Mr Darcy?

> He has very good manors.

English

What do you think of the way Elizabeth behaves in *Pride and Prejudice* on meeting Mr Darcy for the first time?

She acts very a loaf.

Write about the importance of animals in *Of Mice and Men*.

The mice are very important - without them you'd only have the men.

What makes Atticus Finch such a memorable character in *To Kill A Mockingbird*?

His unusual name.

William Wordsworth's famous poem 'I Wandered Lonely as a Cloud' has a simple, uplifting message. What is it?

Clouds get lonely too.

Explore the significance of trust in *Animal Farm*.

Never trust a communist.

Subject: **Literary Criticism**

Use the word 'judicious' in a sentence to illustrate its meaning.

I am using 'judicious' in this sentence to illustrate its meaning

Why should we be optimistic about the future? Use either a discursive or an argumentative style in composing your answer.

Because if you're not positive about the future then you ain't got much hope have you.

Imagine you work for a travel agent. Describe a place you have been to and explain why it would interest someone of a similar age.

My mum and dad drag me to Butlins every year. I wouldn't recommend it to anyone my age.

In what sort of writing would it be appropriate to use bullet points?

Aggressive writing.

What aspects of a text would structuralist critics look at?

The buildings.

Name one key plot device you might find in a comedy of manners.

A person who does not say 'please' and 'thank you'.

List two ways *Pride and Prejudice* can be read.

1. Sitting down, book on lap.
2. Lying down.

What conventions might show a text to be a historical novel?

Historical novels are famous novels

What does it mean when we say a novel is written in the third-person perspective?

There are only three characters.

Define an epistolary novel.

A novel about religious people.

Name two literary genres.

Fiction and non-fiction.

Write a sentence containing a 'question tag'.

I should know what it is, shouldn't I?

Define dialect.

Dr Who's biggest enemies were the dialects.

When people from a particular class share a way of speaking it is called:

Being northern/being southern.

What do we mean by 'mode'?

Grass that's been cut.

Give an example of a sentence with slang in it.

This is an example of a sentence with slang innit.

What are anecdotes an example of?

medicine that you give
someone to stop them
dying of poison

What is a sonnet?

WHAT A MOMMET AND A
POPPET GIVE BIRTH TO.

When writing to argue, what techniques might you use to gain the readers' attention?

Writing in CAPITAL
LETTERS

You should always end a piece of argumentative writing by:

Telling the reader you will slap them if they refuse to agree.

What sort of newspaper article explores opinion rather than facts?

Most.

Give two stylistic features of a column.

GRECIAN. ROMAN.

What does a 'call to action' mean?

When you get made
to go to war.

Give two techniques writers use to create atmosphere.

A few drinks.
Some good friends.

Why should an author keep their audience in mind?

Because if they kept
them in real life that
would be kidnapping.

Give the correct opening for writing a formal letter to a person you don't know.

Opening: 'Who are you?'

What effect can a rhetorical question have?

Irritation

What is a strap line?

When you get sunburnt wearing a strappy top and have white lines on your shoulders.

What is a headline?

The line on your head where your hat was too tight.

What is the purpose of writing to advise?

You can tell people what to do and they can't say no.

What is the effect of imperatives?

They make you poo

When might you use a conditional phrase?

when washing your hair, after
the shampoo phrase.

Give two examples of presentational devices.

Smart board. Pointer

GAP stands for:

fashionable clothes at
affordable prices.

Define 'embody'.

The thing beneath
Em's head.

← Emhead
← Embody

Define 'discourse marker'.

If you get any on your
clothes while you're writing
with it, it will wash off.

What does PEE stand for?

It's like pee, but when
you're really desperate.

Give an example of a 'purpose'.

They're quite like dolphins.

Define ambiguity.

The point of ambiguity is that it can't be defined.

Using the works you have studied, give an example of a heroic couplet.

BATMAN & ROBIN.

What is a roundel?

Similar to a squarel...
but circle shaped.

Give an example of a poetic form.

A poet's driving licence application.

What effect can alliteration have?

Makes the streets
look untidy.

Give an example of a simile.

THIS IS ONE!

What is the technique called when a writer uses the weather to reflect how characters are feeling?

Pathetic falafel

What is poetic meter?

One hundred centimetres
of poem.

Give ONE example of a famous ode.

Ode cologne.

Define physical theatre.

A building, normally quite
big, with a stage and
seats and an expensive
bar.

What is 'Commedia dell'arte'?

It's a high-class sitcom.

When might an author use 'anti-climax'?

It's to be used with anti-freeze.

In poetry, what is the 'voice'?

Someone who reads it out loud.

What is a stanza?

Italian book stand

What is an epitaph?

A swear word.

Define repertoire.

When you keep saying the same thing over and over and over.

English

What themes are important to a Modernist poet?

Technology.

What is a canto?

Faster than a trot.

What made Imagist poets different to other poets writing at the time?

They drew pictures instead of writing words.

Subject: Grammar, Spelling and Punctuation

English

When would a dash be used?

When you're in a rush.

In what circumstances would you employ a semicolon?

When they have a good C.V. and interview.

What are pronouns?

People in favour of nouns

Which sentence is correct?

a) Please tell Damien if there are less than five books in the library.

b) Please tell Damien if there are fewer than five books in the library.

Neither, libraries should always have more than five books.

Name the three tenses.

Stressed, worried and concerned.

Give an example of a sentence containing a suffix.

Suffix to say, I won't be going back there again.

English

What is a subordinate clause?

It's a very meek clause.

Give a brief definition of a split infinitive.

When two people break up and never get back together.

Write a sentence containing a double negative.

Mike is ugly and he smells.

If someone refers to an idiolect, what do they mean?

The opposite of intellect.

When would you use a preposition?

When you want to marry someone.

Give an example of a connective.

Glue, Blu-tack or Sellotape.

Give an example of form.

The one you fill in to get your
National Insurance card.

On average, how many words a minute do we usually speak?

It varies depending on how annoying
you are.

How significant is tone of voice when communicating?

My mum says 'it's not
what you said it's the
way that you said it.'

Give an example of a request and a gesture you might use to emphasise it.

Get lost please.

What effect does eye contact have when you are talking to someone?

It makes them think you fancy them.

What are we referring to when we refer to the 'Queen's English'?

We're referring to the fact that the Queen is English (and a bit German).

Define sociolect.

A violent and dangerous individual with no empathy.

Give an example of a regional accent.

Oo arr missis

Explain the meaning of the word 'dystopia'.

I had dystopia once after eating a bad burger.

Explain what a colon is. Demonstrate how it should be applied in a sentence.

It's a kind of perfume for men. You spray it on your neck to make yourself small nice.

What are adjectives?

Jectives that have been added on.

Write a sentence which includes an oxymoron.

My friend Sam is big, tall and silly;
he's a bit of an oxymoron.

What is the difference between a colon and a semicolon?

These are also known as the large intestine
and the small intestine.
The difference is mainly size.

Subject: Social Science

I think, therefore...

IN EXAMS

Subject: Psychology

Social Science

Describe what is meant by 'forgetting'.

I can't remember

Explain a religious theory for the existence of the world.

The big bang was God dropping something

Outline with two examples what is meant by 'unanswered prayers'.

1 Not winning The Lottery

2 Arsenal never winning the league

 IN EXAMS

Explain the psycho-dynamic approach.

Using your Mind to Move things like a Jedi

Suggest a way to abate aggression.

If your hands are tied behind your back you can't punch people

Express the term 'stereotype'.

It is what kind of CD player you own.

Social Science

What does the phrase 'case study' mean?

It is a process whereby you sit and stare at your suitcase before you go on holiday but not knowing what to pack.

Please fill in the sections of Maslow's Hierarchy of Needs below.

Who said 'I think, therefore I am'?

I did.

What are the benefits of participant observation?

Great, if you are nosy.

What is event sampling?

Going to lots of events to
see what they're like

Social Science

What is an EEG and what is it used for?

It's a food used for scrambling in cooked breakfasts or cold in sandwiches.

How can quantitative data be more useful than qualitative?

There is more of it.

What assumptions does the developmental approach make?

That you will develop mental problems eventually.

What strengths does the psychodynamic approach have?

DYNAMISM

What can MRI scans be used to measure?

The length of an MRI

Social Science

How reliable are the methods of measuring stress?

Not very - if you're stressed you'll probably not take very accurate measurements.

Outline the Oedipus complex.

Explain a psychological technique for managing stress.

Punching your pillow

What is a dependent variable?

One that can't be left alone.

What problems are there with the self-report method of data collection?

People are liars.

Social Science

What ethical issues might arise regarding an experiment involving children?

Children can't be trusted.

What is a snapshot study?

When you examine a photograph.

What does 'diffusion of responsibility' mean?

Giving your work to someone else.

 IN EXAMS

What are the three levels or parts of the mind, according to Sigmund Freud?

Willies, bottoms and boobies.

According to Sigmund Freud, what are the id, the ego and the superego?

Types of action hero.

What does CBT stand for?

Constant Brain Tension.

Give two symptoms of depression.

Being dented and bent in.

In counselling, what does 'setting boundaries' mean?

Building yourself a little wall.

How many hemispheres are there in the brain?

The southern and the northern.

What is a placebo?

A band name

Give an example of 'learned helplessness'.

When you don't know what
the teacher's talking about.

Why are our memories often unreliable?

Because they're fuzzy and vague.

Social Science

What is the hormone that is released when we hug or kiss a loved one?

Passion.

What is a Rorschach inkblot test and what is it used for?

Testing ink pens.

There are five different types of electrical patterns in the brain. Delta waves, for example, are dominant during deep sleep. Name one other brainwave and state when it occurs.

Tidal waves when you dream about the sea.

Subject: **Sociology**

What would be one way of selecting a sample of school children? What would be the advantages and disadvantages of this method?

Choosing the tallest ones.
No disadvantages –
they all have a better
vantage point.

What do sociologists mean by the term 'the hidden curriculum'?

When the teacher
loses their lesson plan.

What is meant by 'domestic roles'?

An actor who gets
typecast as a cleaner

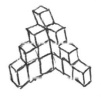

Give one reason why a university student would work and study at the same time.

BECAUSE STUDYING ON ITS OWN IS REALLY BORING.

How would a child's education be affected by growing up in poverty?

They would learn how to bargain hunt.

Give one reason why someone would not vote in a general election.

THEY MIGHT ONLY WANT TO VOTE IN A SPECIFIC ELECTION

Social Science

What is functionalist theory?

The opposite of dysfunctionalist theory.

What is a disadvantage of using official statistics?

You can't make things up.

What is meant by the term fieldwork?

IT IS WHAT THE PEOPLE WHO CAN'T BAT OR BOWL DO IN ROUNDERS

What sources are there for social and ethnic stereotypes?

Tomato ketchup in the South, brown sauce in the North.

What overlap is there between the beliefs of Feminism and Marxism?

ism.

In sociology, what does Action theory state?

NO MATTER HOW MANY BADDIES ARE SHOOTING AT HIM, THE HERO NEVER DIES

Social Science

Give an example of a social norm?

Having coffee with friends

Argue for one side of the nature vs nurture debate.

I argue for this side ↗

Discuss the changing nature of social class.

It changes every year as we get older e.g. we'll be in year 8 next year.

What is social closure?

When the local pub has a
lock in.

What are the key features of Weberian theory?

What significance does differential achievement have
in the UK educational system?

It's different for different people

How does Neo-Marxism differ from Marxism?

Its followers all wear brightly coloured clothes.

Subject: History

Subject: **Political History**

What was introduced in the Children's Charter of 1908?

Children

Where was the American Declaration of Independence signed?

At the bottom.

Name Britain's highest award for bravery.

Probably Nelson's Column

Upon ascending the throne the first thing Queen Elizabeth II did was to...

Sit down

Name one of Abraham Lincoln's greatest achievements?

Having his face carved in rock

Summarise the major events of the Cold War.

It started off by someone throwing an ice cream + then someone threw a lolly back.

Why was the Berlin Wall built?

Germany was competing with China.

What was the largest threat to world peace in the 1980s?

Heavy metal, because it was very loud.

Name three members of the League of Nations.

Arsenal, AC Milan and Bayern.

How might the outcome of Hitler and Chamberlain's meeting at Bad Godesberg have been improved?

It could've been held at Good Godesberg.

What was the issue with the League of Nations' Secretariat?

SHE WAS RUBBISH AT FILING.

Why did the British public want more Dreadnoughts?

To balance out the Dreadcrosses

What is the significance of the 1889 German Navy Cabinet?

It had brass handles and a false bottom.

Name two causes of the Cold War.

1. Soldiers with runny noses.
2. Soldiers with coughs.

What was the U2 incident?

The Edge stole Bono's sunglasses.

What do the letters NATO stand for?

Not At The Office

Who were the members of the Big Three?

King Kong, Godzilla and The Hulk.

Give a brief summary of events of the Beagle Conflict.

Many Beagles lost their lives.

History

What was the cause of the Gallic Wars?

A gallic bread shortage.

What were the terms of the Treaty of Versailles?

AUTUMN TERM, SPRING TERM, SUMMER TERM

What was the Crimean War?

A war against criminals.

What were the events of the Fashoda Crisis?

Lots of people turned up to a party in the same dress.

What was the Easter Rising?

The tradition of cooking Hot Cross Buns for Easter.

What were the Swing Rioters of 1830 protesting against?

Jazz.

What was the purpose of the Barebones Parliament?

They provide a skeleton staff when other politicians are on holiday.

What was the position of the Whigs in the eighteenth century?

On top of bald people's heads.

What was the Lytton Commission reporting on?

Picking up rubbish

What factors contributed to the fall of the British Empire?

Everybody got bored of eating fish and chips all the time.

What was Britain's interest in the Suez Canal?

That's where Suez pudding comes from.

For what is the Order of the Garter awarded?

Holding up stockings.

Why were the Corn Laws repealed?

When they were pealed the first time there were bits left on them.

What was Chamberlain's plan for appeasement?

That peas should be served alongside fish and chips.

What event occurred under the Elementary Education Act of 1870?

Sherlock Holmes became required reading in Schools

Name two Dissenting groups.

SUGAR AND GRAVY CUBES
BOTH DISSENT IN WATER

Why was the Pains and Penalties Bill introduced in 1820?

To standardise footballing laws.

What was the Poor Law Act of 1388?

It made it illegal to be poor.

What is the definition of an Oligarchy?

A Society where ugly people are in charge.

Name one of the main principles behind Chartism.

It's an unreasonable fear of charts.

What is the Revolution of 1668 also sometimes known as?

The Goriest Revolution.

Subject: _Social History_

Summarise the key developments of the Industrial Revolution.

Industry revolved

Who were the Bolsheviks?

People. led by linen

Explain what is meant by the word 'dictator'.

Someone who reads
out loud

233

Why did Britons have better health after the year 1990?

Because the eighties were
over

Name two of the classes which existed in Medieval
England.

History class &
Geography class

What was the cause of the Hungarian Revolution in 1956?

THEY WERE GETTING HUNGARIER AND HUNGARIER

What problem rocked the USSR in 1986?

The Beatles

What is hyperinflation?

When a bouncy castle is blown up so much if you jumped on it it would burst

What is Appel Quay famous for?

Opening Appel Door.

What happens when a country demilitarises?

Its citizens lose motivation and feel low.

Name the five Giants of Poverty.

Jolly Green Giant, BFG, Hagrid, Beanstalk Giant & Gulliver.

What was the subject of the Beveridge report?

Hot drinks

What, or who, were the Suffragettes?

60's pop group

Give a brief description of the 'never-never'.

Where Peter Pan lives.

What is public health?

Anything involving eating apples outdoors or running in parks.

What is a census?

Latin for a hundred.

What was the Special Areas Act?

Something very rude.

What was the purpose of the labour exchange?

So people could try each other's jobs for a while.

Give a consequence of the General Strike.

There were no Generals to run the army.

Give a brief description of the events of 'Red Friday'.

It followed 'Really Sunny But No Sun Cream Thursday'.

What is Social Engineering?

Inventions like Facebook and Twitter.

What was said to be the last defence against extreme poverty?

Winning the lottery.

What were the consequences of the 1765 Stamp Act?

Fair postage for all.

How did the flying shuttle revolutionise the textile industry?

They could use new materials from space.

What was the Wall Street Crash?

A CAR MOUNTED THE PAVEMENT $ HIT THE WALL

What is another name for the 'Roaring Twenties'?

The shouting Post-Teens.

Give a definition of a co-operative society.

A VILLAGE OF PEOPLE THAT
LIKE TO SHOP AT THEIR LOCAL
STORE.

What sort of engine was the table engine?

It keeps your food warm.

What were the events leading up to the St Valentine's Day Massacre?

Someone didn't get
any cards.

Who were the Bolsheviks?

A Russian ballet company.

Who was the last tsar of Russia?

Tsar Nicholas the Last.

Subject: *Cultural History*

History

How did Christopher Columbus discover America?

While he was cursing about the Atlantic

What did Mahatma Gandhi and Genghis Khan have in common?

Unusual names

What does The Statue of Liberty represent?

A green lady holding up a large glass of wine She is wearing a crown. She is the Queen of America.

What makes November 5 a significant date in history?

The rhyme tells us to remember it.

In regards to Henry VIII, what is the rhyme 'divorced, beheaded, died, divorced, beheaded, survived' about?

Death, divorce and survival.

How did William the Conqueror get his moniker?

He went to the opticians.

Name two advantages Oliver Cromwell's New Model
Army had over Charles I's Royalists.

They were plastic so
they never got hurt.

What was the purpose of the Domesday Book?

People in olden times were quite
superstitious and they would
predict the end of the world.

What was the role of the Lord Protector?

Protecting the lord

What was the War of the Roses regarding?

Trying to stop the greenfly eating them.

For what reason was James I also known as James VI?

They couldn't count.

Name two attributed qualities of Richard the Lionheart.

He had long flowing hair and sharp teeth.

How did King Cnut reprove his courtiers?

He cnutted them.

Who were the Princes in the Tower?

Rapunzel and Sleeping Beauty are two Princes that lived in a tower.

What was Hugh Despenser's place in the court of Edward II?

Giving out snacks and cold drinks.

What was the House of Tudor?

It had a white front with black beams and low doors.

Against who did Robert the Bruce defend Scotland?

Macbeth.

Why was James II known as the Great Pretender?

He was the most talented member of the Pretenders.

Why was George IV called the 'first gentleman of England'?

He always put the toilet seat down.

What was the Crystal Palace?

Football Team

Name the four humours of Greek medicine.

Slapstick, irony, wordplay and poo jokes.

In Ancient Greece, where did the clinical observation of a patient with an illness begin?

At the doctor's

What was Vegetius famous for?

His healthy diet.

In Medieval England, what was a reredorter?

Someone who comes in to decorate after the first time goes wrong.

What is the Hippocratic Oath?

An oath you don't intend to keep.

What is the definition of a 'quack' doctor?

One that specialises in ducks.

Who was the Ancient Egyptian God of Death?

A newbie.

Who were the visigoths?

Fans of The Cure

List three notable features of Gaulish society.

Asterix, Obelix and Cacofonix.

What language did the Romans write in?

Roman.

History

What was the significance of Hadrian's Wall?

It was the first ever wall.

Name one characteristic of the Enlightenement.

Brightness.

Describe an Ionic column.

A column that's deliberately contrary to its expected meaning.

What technological advances did Rome bring to Britain?

Roman candles.

What are Picts an example of?

A tool for mining.

What is the Upper Palaeolithic?

A dinosaur's thigh bone.

Explain the reason for the erection of the Berlin Wall.

To hold up the Berlin Ceiling

Berlin Ceiling

Berlin Window

Berlin Wall

Explain the dangers of life as a cowboy in the American Midwest.

High risk of being shot by Clint Eastwood.

Subject: **Business Studies**

How do the following companies fund themselves?

a) BBC   phone-in competitions

b) ITV   same as the above

Explain the phrase 'free press'.

When your mum irons
    trousers for you.

Explain the word 'wholesaler'.

Someone who sells you whole
items, e.g. a whole cake.

Paul frequently uses the internet to research information. Suggest two items of information Paul could locate on the internet which might help him in running his business.

Item 1: www. how-to-run-a-business. com

Item 2: www. how-not-to-run-a-business. com

Suggest three steps Paul is likely to take when selecting the best candidate for a job.

Step one: **You're hired**

Step two: **You're fired**

Step three: **You're hired**

Assess Fashion House plc's choice to locate its factory near Birmingham. Is Birmingham the right location for this type of business?

No. People from Birmingham aren't very fashionable.

Describe the term 'stakeholder'.

A vampire hunter.
Buffy being the most famous

Hugo King is an engineer. He is a sole trader. Explain the business term 'sole trader'.

It means he has sold his sole to the devil!

What is a 'partnership'?

A Ship that takes two people to drive

John's net pay is £150. His deductions are £38.
a) Work out John's gross pay.

The money he spends on porn magazines every week.

b) State one mandatory deduction from John's pay.

Beer

c) State one voluntary deduction John may or may not pay.

Tax

Business Subjects

Claire used good body language at a job interview.
Can you think of three examples of good body language
that Claire may have used.

1 pole dancing
2 The moonwalk
3 The Bolero

Claire was well prepared for her interview.
Explain how Claire may have prepared herself for the
interview.

Had a bath and put on her
lucky pants.

How does 'fair trade' benefit others?

It stops people getting beaten
up in the playground.

What is an ISA?

She's a cute girl in my class.

What does APR mean?

It's a short way of writing April.

What is a standing order?

"Stand up, now!"

What is the security code on a credit card?

621.

Jane has raised money for a fun day at her school by selling cupcakes at lunchtimes. Give three other ways that she could raise money.

1. Put the money in stacks
2. Put it on shelves
3. Hold it up high

Name one important piece of equipment needed to set up a wireless network.

A rooster

The fun day requires a risk assessment before it can go ahead. What is a risk assessment?

Too risky to say.

What does 'fair trade' mean?

When you swap your best comic for a really rare action figure

It's the day of the fun day. What are the ways that Jane can assess whether it has been a success?

Ask people if they had fun, and count the bodies.

Subject: **Government & Politics**

Why do some people participate in democracy more than others?

Because only some people
are politicians.

What is a nation-state?

A country that's in a
bad state.

Why might global corporations be considered more powerful than governments?

THEY OWN THE GLOBE
WHEREAS GOVERNMENTS OWN
COUNTRIES

What is meant by the term 'federal' state?

A place where everyone has to wear a hat.

What are the benefits of a pluralist democracy?

Two heads are better than one!

What is the difference between the executive and the legislature?

The executive runs the company, the legislature is the rules.

What beliefs are common to those who are classed as Eurosceptics?

They don't think
Europe exists.

Explain the meaning of the term 'sovereignty'.

When you drop a ring in your tea.

What part does the House of Lords play in legislative procedure?

IT KEEPS THE PEOPLE INVOLVED
IN THE PROCEDURE WARM AND
DRY.

What effect does devolution have on the way the UK is governed?

It means it's governed by Monkeys!

In US politics, what does the term 'impeachment' mean?

It's like imprisonment, but with fruit.

In what way does the US constitution restrict the government's actions?

THEY HAVE A WEAK CONSTITUTION AND SO CAN'T TAKE MUCH EXERCISE

If a government is given a mandate, what does this mean? How might this come about?

A mandate is a boys' night out. A womandate is a girls' night out.

What caused the increase in labour mobility within the EU?

More exercise.

What changes would a codified UK constitution bring about?

More people eating cod.

What effect does a strong judiciary have on civil liberties?

Judiciary overpowers liberties, because they are too polite.

Explain the relationship between the US Senate, House of Representatives and the president.

They get on really well.

What government policies would be considered to assist or hinder multiculturalism?

Assist: helpful policies
Hinder: Unhelpful Policies.

Outline the basic difference between left-wing and right-wing political beliefs.

It's all about which side you're sat on.

In what ways is the 'first past the post' electoral system undemocratic?

It's not fair to people who can't run very fast

Who sits in the Council of the European Union?

Saruman.

What arguments are used against international aid?

IT'S NOT AS NICE AS CHERRYADE

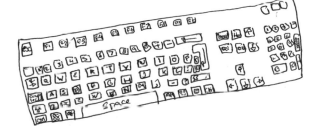

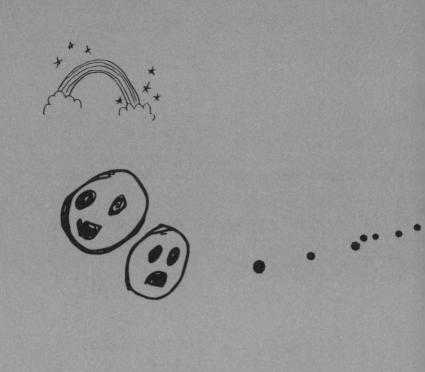

Subject: **The Arts**

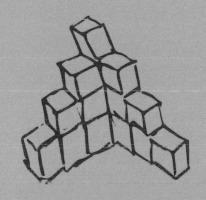

Subject: **Media Studies**

Give an example of a media product aimed at a niche audience.

The Antiques Roadshow app.

What does 'self-regulation' mean in the context of media industries?

Deciding not to watch a whole series in one go on Netflix.

Explain how a media star can promote themselves using the internet.

Putting a naked selfie on Instagram is a good way.

Explain the importance of niche markets to media industries.

They're where media people buy
Statues and other knick-knacks.

Give an example of 'invasion of privacy' in the context of media industries.

Big Brother

What are the important qualities of a successful soap opera?

1. Being screened during the day.

2. A big enough student population to stay at home and watch it.

What are the vital ingredients for a successful action film?

1. Bruce Willis
2. Explosions
3. Car chases

Give a two-sentence pitch for your action film idea.

The lead actor is Bruce Willis. There are explosions and car chases.

How can live streaming of reality shows cause legal problems for its producers?

If somebody dies during the show it suddenly turns into dead streaming, which is horrible for everyone.

Suggest three ways to promote a new soap opera.

1. Give away free soap.
2. Give away free opera tickets.
3. include plenty of sex scenes.

How do television companies conduct research into their audiences?

With cameras inside TVs.

The Arts

Why is sound such a powerful film technique?

Because silent movies are so 1920s.

In film editing, what is Fade In/Fade Out?

It's to do with the fashion
in denim jeans worn in the film.

What is the function of continuity in TV and film?

It allows you to keep watching Netflix
for hours without having to move.

The media industry is 'self-regulated'. what does this mean?

It controls its own alcohol intake.

Why are 'niche' audiences important for media producers?

Because lots of audiences watch films in alcoves.

What is a broadsheet newspaper?

The opposite of narrow sheet papers.

The Arts

What is copyright and how long does it last?

A law that lasts as
long as the copy is right.

Give two examples of products aimed at a 'niche' audience.

Small sofas or armchairs.

Why are eBooks becoming increasingly popular?

Because any word with an 'e' in front
of it looks cool.

What is an indie author?

An author who is into indie music.

What is a retweet?

Singing back a bird's call.

What are the main advantages of a music magazine being available on the internet?

There aren't any because you can't and listen to YouTube clips at the same time.

Subject:  Music

What is meant by the term 'a cappella'?

A smaller than normal hat.

Give an example of a song cycle in classical music.

'There are 9 million
bicycles in Beijing'
by Katie Melua

What are the main features of baroque music?

It can't be fixed.

Give an example of a sonata. What makes your example a sonata?

Frank Sonata. He was a born Sonata.

What are the components of a diminished seventh chord?

Fewer than the components of a whole seventh chord

What are the four groups of an orchestra?

Drums, strings, wood and wind.

What is a fugue?

Someone who is on the run from the police.

Explain the chromatic scale and give an example of its use in music.

The chromatic scale is a brightly coloured scale measuring everything from red through to purple

In music terms, what is a vamp?

Are you telling me there's a Twilight musical? OMG.

The Arts

When a score instructs you to play an arpeggio, what does this mean?

It's getting a bit too big for its boots.

What are the key differences between a waltz and a march?

A waltz is a type of dance. A march is what soldiers do.

What is the Italian term for a change of speed in music?

Fast-a, fast-a

What is the effect of a change of key?

New locks

What is ground bass?

GRINDED UP FISH

Explain the idea of homophony.

A cake house.

What are the main features of a Scots ballad?

Indistinguishable lyrics.

How does a mezzo soprano differ from a soprano?

One has cheese on it.

How would you recognise a walking bass?

Explain what a pentatonic scale is and give an example of its use.

It is an instrument used in devil worship.

What is pizzicato?

Part of an Italian cat.

Define the term 'atonal'.

Something that goes on forever.

The Arts

Give examples of instruments you would find in the percussion section of an orchestra.

Blunt instruments.

What are the benefits of an ensemble over a solo performer?

If one's really bad, the others can cover it up.

What is a leitmotiv?

The opposite of a heavy motive.

What piece of equipment can be used in situations where a stringed instrument can't be tuned by ear?

An electronic tuna

Who sang the soul songs 'Respect' and 'Think'?

Urethra Franklin

What musical structure is commonly found in classical music by composers such as Mozart and Beethoven?

A sympathy.

The Arts

What do you understand by the terms 'homophonic' and 'polyphonic'?

One doesn't like gay people and the other doesn't like parrots.

What is 'a cappella'?

A small Italian hat.

To which family of instruments does the clarinet belong?

Clarinets are part of the wind-producing family.

What is a riff?

A thing Elizabethans wore round their necks.

What is the time signature of this extract?

Subject: **DraMa**

What is the importance of the performer in modern theatre?

It would be a really boring play without any actors.

Discuss the effect of theatre technology in one contemporary piece.

Robots aren't very emotive

Analyse the role of the director in modern theatre.

THE ROLE OF THE DIRECTOR IS TO DIRECT, LIKE THE ROLE OF THE ACTOR IS TO ACT

The Arts

What effect do the comic characters in Shakespeare's non-comic plays have?

They ruin the mood.

What elements of a play could be evaluated and developed as it is created?

The bad bits.

Give an example of an effective use of staging.

Successfully building a stage

Discuss what is most important out of lighting, sound and costume.

Costume, unless it is a nudist play.

In stage lighting, what is gel?

A slimy substance.

What is meant by the terms 'protagonist' and 'antagonist'?

A protagonist is for agonists and an antagonist is against them

What elements should be included in a stage ground plan?

A stage, the ground.

What is a monologue?

When one person won't shut up.

Give an example of a way body language can be used to portray emotion.

Putting your fingers up at somebody when you are annoyed.

In *King Lear*, what theme is most present when Edmund says, 'The wheel is come full circle'?

> Car Maintenance.

Write about the character in *Romeo and Juliet* for whom you have the most sympathy.

> I have most sympathy for the audience

What advice would you give an actor playing Romeo?

> It's just a teenage crush - youill get over it.

How does Dylan Thomas present Willy Nilly in *Under Milk Wood*?

He keeps him in his trousers.

Write about two characters who have power in Arthur Miller's *The Crucible*.

All of the witches have magical powers.

Subject: ..............P.E...

Name ONE factor that will increase sports participation.

Increased sports.

What national facilities does Sport England run?

Sports facilities.

What will concessions mean for some groups at sports facilities?

Admitting defeat.

Name a common advantage for a country hosting a world sporting event.

They can stay at their own houses

What aspect of Rugby League changed in order to meet the needs of television?

Everyone got their hair done

What pressure resulted in the introduction of the tie-break in tennis?

FROM PLAYERS PULLING ON THE UMPIRE'S TIE TOO HARD

What influences can encourage good sporting behaviour amongst young people?

Scary P.E. teachers.

What name is given to an unpaid participant in sport?

Slave.

How often are the Olympic games held?

Every 400 years.

What is the name given to the physical activity which improves health and fitness?

Playing the Wii.

What sport requires flexibility?

Limbo dancing.

What is the purpose rules serve in sport?

They make sure the lines at the edges of the pitches are straight.

In cricket, what is referred to as a 'delayed dead ball'?

Someone reacting slowly to being hit in the crotch.

What factors can make a competition balanced?

Holding your arms out straight and staring at a spot on the wall.

What must sportspeople do before taking part in a sports activity?

Get to where the sports activity is taking place

PE

What skill is required by sprinters?

Big legs.

What qualities does a good referee possess?

A strong whistle.

Who plans the strategies for a team?

Mr ~~T~~ Hannibal

315

In athletics, name three types of jumping event.

High jump
Long jump
Tripe jump

What sports category do skateboarding, scootering and surfing fall into?

Bored sports.

What must you do after exercising to prevent muscle damage?

Worm down.

Give examples of 'anaerobic activity'.

Zumba is an aerobic
activity. So is Boxercise

What effects can excess weight have on the body?

Heaviness.
It makes you fat.

Give reasons why exercise helps a person lose weight.

They are so busy
exercising they
have no time to
eat cake.

What is a person's metabolic rate?

I would have thought only robots have metal bolics.

What is the Fartlek training method?

It consists of parts and Daleks.

What two qualities are important in order to be an effective sports coach?

Wheels and comfortable seats.

PE

Explain two ways in which an amateur sportsperson can secure funding.

1. Theft.

2. Bribery.

Give three examples of active leisure activities.

PlayStation, Xbox, Wii

If you're interested in finding out more about our books, find us on Facebook at **Summersdale Publishers** and follow us on Twitter at @**Summersdale**.

www.summersdale.com